D0753200

CAJUN

MARDI GRAS

MASKS

Folk Art and Artists Series
Michael Owen Jones
General Editor

Books in this series focus on the work of informally trained or self-taught artists rooted in regional, occupational, ethnic, racial, or gender-specific traditions. Authors explore the influence of artists' experiences and aesthetic values upon the art they create, the process of creation, and the cultural traditions that served as inspiration or personal resource. The wide range of art forms featured in this series reveals the importance of aesthetic expression in our daily lives and gives striking testimony to the richness and vitality of art and tradition in the modern world.

CAJUN MARDI GRAS MASKS

Carl Lindahl and Carolyn Ware

University Press of Mississippi   Jackson

Photo credits: Linda Adams, 91 (top); Barry Jean Ancelet, 13 (right), 22, 32, 33, 35 (right), 42, 65, 68, 70 (bottom), 78, 79 (right), 86, 90 (top), 93 (top), 95; Mary Caroline Ancelet, 63; Carl Lindahl, 8, 10 (bottom), 11, 14, 17, 21, 27 (right), 29, 38, 39, 43, 45, 47, 48, 49, 50, 51, 52, 53, 54, 57, 58, 60, 61, 62, 66 (bottom), 72 (bottom), 73, 74, 76, 79 (left), 80, 81, 82, 87 (right); Ann Arlosoroff Vise Nunes, 19, 28 (bottom), 72 (top), 88, 92; Maida Owens, 27 (left), 59, 75, 83, 87 (left), 90 (bottom); Lauren C. Post collection, 18; Helena Putnam, 12, 13 (left), 15, 24, 31, 35 (left), 44, 64; Ronnie Roshto and Georgie Manuel, 34; Carolyn Ware, 9, 10, above, 25, 26, 28 (top), 70 (top), 84, 85, 91 (bottom), 93 (bottom), 94

The paper in this book meets the guidelines for permanence and durability of the Committee on Production Guidelines for Book Longevity of the Council on Library Resources.

Library of Congress Cataloging-in-Publication Data

Lindahl, Carl.
    Cajun Mardi Gras masks / Carl Lindahl and Carolyn Ware.
        p.   cm. — (Folk art and artists series)
    Includes bibliographical references.
    ISBN 0-87805-968-7 (cloth : alk. paper). — ISBN 0-87805-969-5 (paper : alk. paper)
    1. Masks—Louisiana—Basile. 2. Masks—Louisiana—Tee Mamou. 3. Carnival—Louisiana—Basile. 4. Carnival—Louisiana—Tee Mamou. 5. Cajuns—Louisiana—Basile—Social life and customs. 6. Cajuns—Louisiana—Tee Mamou—Social life and customs. I. Ware, Carolyn.
II. Title. III. Series.
    GT1748.U52L85 1997
    391.4'34'09763—dc21   97-11388
                                CIP

British Library Cataloging-in-Publication data available

To the Mardi Gras communities of Basile and Tee Mamou

CONTENTS

CAJUN MARDI GRAS AND MASK-MAKING

Tee Mamou Mardi Gras
sing their traditional
begging song in French
while crawling, 1996.

YOU ARE WATCHING from your porch, a live chicken cradled in your arms. You stare up the road, but you hear them before you see them—a chorus of high-pitched whoops and wordless yells ringing over the music. A line of trucks comes into view, in its center a long, high-sided wagon filled with color—costumed arms draped over the sideboards and dozens of masked faces with giant unblinking eyes that seem to stare at you. As the truckful of faces pulls to a halt on the road before your yard, the music stops, the whooping subsides, and an unmasked man, a whip in one hand and a white flag in the other, walks across the yard to you.

Tee Mamou women's Mardi Gras wagon full of maskers, 1995.

"*Le Mardi Gras demande votre permission pour visiter ta maison*" ("the Mardi Gras asks your permission to visit your house"). You nod assent, the caped man waves his flag in the air, and the truck suddenly empties, the swarm of screened faces closing in—until dozens of them are pressed against the porch where you are standing. Everything you see is blinding, moving color. Your neighbors and relatives are out there somewhere, behind the masks.

The maskers sing a begging song in French, repeating the words "*mon cher*" or "*mon cher camarade*"—"my dear," "my dear friend." Are they singing to you or to each other?

The song ends with a chorus of yells, and the music begins again. Unmasked mu-sicians strike up a tune on accordion and fiddle and the maskers begin waltzing with each other. One breaks out of the dance and begins climbing the pillars of your porch; another pulls your sister off the porch and into the swirl; a third grabs your daughter and runs away with her. Two more have taken a wheelbarrow out of your shed and are pushing it in crazy circles through the yard, while a third one sits in the wheelbarrow laughing and screaming; the *capitaine* pursues them, lashing their backs and legs with his whip. One Mardi Gras comes up to you and tries to grab the chicken out of your hands, saying, "*Quelle belle poule*" ("What a pretty chicken").

You stare into the small holes of the

9

10

Far left, above:
Tee Mamou Mardi Gras
Renée Frugé scales the
front porch of her host's
house, 1994.

Far left, below:
Basile's Mardi Gras
descend upon a house,
1996.

With their fists in the
air as they sing the Mardi
Gras song, Basile maskers
close in on a house, 1996.

C'est dur, ça: Basile reveler strikes an unsettling pose, staring into photographer's lens, 1992.

12

Above:
Mardi Gras runs off with
Tee Mamou child.

Left:
Basile Mardi Gras running
off with their host's
wheelbarrow, 1992.

13

reveler's screen-wire mask, trying to deter-mine the identity of the would-be thief. "Is that you, Ron?"

A distorted, high-pitched voice answers, "*C'est dur, ça, quand le Mardi Gras connait toi, et tu connais pas le Mardi Gras*" ("It's tough, isn't it, when the Mardi Gras knows who you are, but you don't know the Mardi Gras").

The Mardi Gras mask is both treasure and necessity, essential to the celebration of the most important day of the year for many of the Cajuns who inhabit the farms and small prairie towns of southwest Loui-siana. There are in fact several rural com-munities where, partly because of laws that prohibit citizens from concealing their faces, face paint has replaced masking altogether. Also, for many Mardi Gras en-thusiasts, the two-piece Mardi Gras suits and the tall, pointed *capuchons*, or Mardi Gras hats, are just as important as the masks. But to those Cajuns—particularly the older ones—who believe that the idea of a Mardi Gras costume is to help celebrants disguise their identities so thor-oughly that even their relatives and closest friends won't know them, the traditional screen-wire mask provides the greatest challenge and, potentially, the greatest rewards of disguise.

The loose-fitting Mardi Gras suit, often sewn with great care, is neverthe-less almost a uniform, calculated to make

all guisers look alike, to the point that ob-servers cannot even distinguish males from females. Similarly, the *capuchons*, elaborate as they may be, perform, like the suits, the twin purposes of concealment and adorn-ment. But the screen mask is more reveal-ing: it obscures but does not fully hide the most intimate and personal part of the body, the face. This partial covering allows a distorted view of eyes, nose, and chin to those who come close to the mask. Hence Mardi Gras revelers are forced to employ varied and creative kinds of ornamenta-tion—painting the screen wire and fringing the mask with yarn, or even covering it with fabric—as well as to use their acting abilities to render themselves mysteriously strange to the people who know them best. With and behind their masks, Mardi Gras revelers create new, play selves.

Among today's Mardi Gras participants, masks still serve for many as the most vital element of disguise, but some participants

Half-face mask made by J. B. LeBlue bears a sur-face resemblance to New Orleans-style masks. Basile, 1990.

14

become so attached to a particular mask—because of its comfort, its beauty, or its significance as a family heirloom—that they wear it year after year, ironically transforming it from a disguise to an indelible badge of personal identity.

Mardi Gras masks thus fill the sometimes contradictory functions of disguise and display. The first mask made by a Mardi Gras guiser may successfully conceal the wearer when it is initially worn, and if, as many maskmakers do, the wearer changes the facial designs or borders from year to year, the mask will continue to fool his or her neighbors. But often a certain mask becomes so closely associated with its wearer that it serves as a second face, making the wearer's identity transparent.

What and Who Are Mardi Gras?

Screen masks are worn once a year, during the day-long celebration of the Cajun country *courir de Mardi Gras*, or Mardi Gras "run," a unique celebration that shares roots with such better-known festivals as the New Orleans Mardi Gras. Both in New Orleans and in Cajun country, Mardi Gras means "Fat Tuesday" and is celebrated traditionally by Catholics as a time to eat lavishly before the onset of Lent. For at least nine centuries, various Christian cultures have enjoyed a period of feasting before beginning the forty-day fast that stretches from Ash Wednesday to Easter Sunday.

For both New Orleanians and Cajuns, Mardi Gras involves not only feasting but also drinking, costumes, processions, and wild behavior. Similar activities occur in the carnivals of Rio, Trinidad, and Venice, which also trace their roots to medieval pre-Lenten celebrations.

Despite a common source, Cajun Mardi Gras differs substantially from the New Orleans celebration, most obviously in terms of scale. In New Orleans, more than a hundred thousand people may

In their Mardi Gras suits, masks, and *capuchons*, males are sometimes almost indistinguishable from females. Basile, 1992.

15

gather to watch a single parade. At a Cajun Mardi Gras, in contrast, the audience is often smaller in number than the group on parade: for example, a family of five and a few neighbors may play host to seventy masked revelers.

There are also differences in the dynamics of procession. New Orleans's urban Mardi Gras involves lavish display along parade routes lined with spectators, whereas Cajun country Mardi Gras, though it often climaxes with a parade through the center of the town where it started, consists mainly of house visits in which a body of costumed revelers—from as few as a dozen to more than one hundred—travel to neighbors' yards. In New Orleans, the crowds come to the parade: in effect they visit the Mardi Gras. In Cajun country, however, the Mardi Gras visits the spectators, carrying its procession right to their front doors.

The New Orleans celebration has influenced some of the larger cities in Cajun country: towns such as Crowley and Lafayette, with populations ranging from ten thousand to ninety thousand, feature parades in which costumed people riding floats throw plastic beads and coins to spectators. But such behavior seldom occurs in the two dozen prairie communities where the country Mardi Gras is celebrated.

The types of costuming and decoration most common in New Orleans Mardi Gras are uncommon in the Cajun enactment. In New Orleans the special Mardi Gras colors—purple, green, and gold (adopted from the liturgical banners used by the Catholic Church to mark the Lenten season)—are ubiquitous, found on costumes, streamers, balloons, and masks. In Cajun country these colors are far less conspicuous. Similarly, the type of mask most commonly associated with New Orleans is the half-face mask; this style is relatively rare among Cajuns. For example, J. B. LeBlue is the only Cajun maskmaker featured in this book who has made a half-face mask, and only a few of his hundreds of masks are of this type; even these few differ from New Orleans masks in having no eyeholes. The Cajun screen-wire mask relies on the same visual principle as the screen window: someone inside a house, if his or her face is close to the window, can see the outside clearly, but people walking past the house cannot always recognize the face of the watcher inside.

For those who have visited both the New Orleans and Cajun enactments, the most striking difference is likely to be the greater intimacy of the Cajun festival. Cajun Mardi Gras participants inevitably induce their audience to interact with them. It is impossible for a "civilian" witnessing a Cajun Mardi Gras to avoid being danced with, begged from, sung at, abducted or teased by at least one of the masked figures. Most Cajun Mardi Gras participants

Above:
Cajun country Mardi Gras spectators easily become participants as the masked revelers dance with their neighbors. Basile, 1992.

Left:
Tee Mamou Mardi Gras sing their traditional begging song in French as they approach the house, 1996.

17

Photos from the 1930s illustrate the importance of horses and feature Mardi Gras masks that are much like those made in Basile and Tee Mamou today.

terre" ("The Mardi Gras, *they* come from England"); in Tee Mamou, "*On vient de l'Angleterre*" ("We come from England"). Finally, Mardi Gras designates individual revelers. A spectator may ask a masker, "What are you doing, Mardi Gras?" Or, at Basile, a reveler may be awarded the title "Best All-Around Mardi Gras."

Two Mardi Gras Communities

No matter where it is celebrated, a vital Mardi Gras takes the shape of its community. Cajun country Mardi Gras is no exception: instead of mob scenes featuring thousands of mutual strangers, as in New Orleans, the Cajun country Mardi Gras features one-on-one interactions between costumed revelers and their undisguised friends and relatives. For all the attention that it has recently received from tourists, Cajun Mardi Gras remains a neighborly affair. Central to its enactment is a house visit in which the familiar is made strange as guisers rely on costuming and role playing to hide their identities from people who know them well; the great majority of Cajun Mardi Gras participants live in the same community that they visit.

Basile and Tee Mamou are two of the most vital and distinctive Cajun Mardi Gras communities. Their centers separated by just seven miles of prairie farm land and crawfish ponds, these neighborhoods border each other; indeed, on Mardi Gras day, the two different bands of guisers follow

have no use for the New Orleans version of their festival: as far as they are concerned, the country Mardi Gras is older, more traditional, more neighborly, and more fun.

Outsiders are often confused by the variety of ways in which Cajuns use the term *Mardi Gras,* which for them carries four distinct meanings. First, for Cajuns and other French-speaking Catholics, Mardi Gras signifies a moveable date in the church calendar, a Tuesday between February 4 and March 11 that marks the eve of Ash Wednesday. Second, for Cajuns and for New Orleanians, Mardi Gras refers to the celebration that unfolds on Ash Wednesday eve.

Third, among Cajuns (but not New Orleanians) "Mardi Gras" names the entire company of maskers who visit houses during the celebration. In Basile, the maskers sing, "*Le Mardi Gras, ça viennent de l'Angle-*

The *capitaine*'s truck leads the Tee Mamou women's Mardi Gras wagon through the country, 1991.

routes that nearly overlap. Although Tee Mamou's Mardi Gras differs substantially from Basile's, the two resemble each other in important ways that set them apart from most other Cajun enactments.

First, there are no horses in either the Basile or the Tee Mamou procession. At most of the Cajun *courirs*—at Mamou and Church Point, for example—flamboyant horsemanship and horseback charges of farmhouses are central to the spectacle. Before World War II, nearly all country *courirs*, including Basile's and Tee Mamou's, were horseback processions. Horses made sense in the village topography of fifty years ago, when most Cajuns inhabited small, closely adjoining farmsteads and could make a horseback circuit of their community with relative speed and ease. But today small family farms are disappearing, leaving the countryside sparsely populated. In Basile, former farmers brought their families to town; in 1995, the Mardi Gras visited thirty-eight homes and businesses, only one of which was in the outlying countryside. In Tee Mamou—which is not a town, but a cluster of rural neighborhoods—most stops remain rural, but they are separated by such great distances that horses cannot visit them all during the

19

eight or nine hours allotted for the *courir*. So horses have disappeared, replaced by enormous wagons that carry the maskers.

Today's Tee Mamou and Basile Mardi Gras do not miss the horses. "It's better with the wagons," says Vories Moreau, who has run Mardi Gras in both communities. "The horses were too much bother; they kept you busy all the time. Now that they're gone, the Mardi Gras can spend more time just being Mardi Gras." Opportunities for clowning, engaging the crowd, and trickery are enhanced now that the Mardi Gras can travel freely on foot without having to tend their horses.

A second way in which Basile and Tee Mamou Mardi Gras resemble each other while differing from most other rural enactments is that both communities celebrate more than one *courir* each year. Unlike such cities as New Orleans and Nice—for which Mardi Gras encompasses a whole season, with two weeks or more of parades, balls, and festivities reaching a crescendo on the day itself—Cajun towns tend to celebrate their Mardi Gras on one day alone. But in both Tee Mamou and Basile, when women, who had been traditionally excluded from running Mardi Gras in most communities, decided to mask, they formed separate *courirs* on the weekend before Fat Tuesday.

The Tee Mamou women's *courir de Mardi Gras* dates to the early 1970s, when a handful of women led by a male captain

traveled the countryside in the back of a farm truck. This first run was well received by the community, which was "just very welcoming," according to its earliest participants. Several years later, the women approached Gerald Frugé, the *capitaine* of the Tee Mamou men's run, about "captaining for" their group, too. Assisted by five or six male cocaptains, Frugé continues as *capitaine* for both runs.

Basile possesses a similar Mardi Gras history. The oldest celebration, all male, took place on Mardi Gras day. When a group of women decided to run as well, they held their celebration the weekend before Mardi Gras. In the early 1980s, as the number of participants dwindled and it became too expensive for the town to support two days of festivities, the men and women decided to run together on Tuesday. Later, Mardi Gras Association members, fearing that children would not want to join the festival when they reached age fifteen, instituted a children's Mardi Gras to spark the interest of the young; it takes place on the preceding Sunday. Still, in Basile, as in Tee Mamou, no masker makes the processional journey to neighbors' houses more than one day a year. This book focuses on the Tuesday mixed male-female run in Basile and the Saturday women's run in Tee Mamou.

Third, Basile and Tee Mamou are among the few Mardi Gras in which the entire group of visitors sings a begging song in

Tony Johnson, left,
and Mike Broussard
demonstrate the range of
masking in Basile, 1992.
The *nègre*, a black-faced
character, is one of the
few who wear face paint;
a larger number wear
rubber masks.

Above:
Tee Mamou screen-wire
mask, 1994.

Left:
Classic Tee Mamou
needlepoint mask, 1988.

French for their hosts at every stop. The Tee Mamou song, sung by the group in unison as they approach the house, describes a bottle being drunk to the dregs; the Mardi Gras says that they will not drink what remains, and then they ask for permission to dance with the host's son. The Basile song, performed after the group has reached the house and is clustered around the host, is sung largely by a leader, usually Potic Rider, but all join in on the chorus, pumping their fists in the air at special times. The Mardi Gras sing that they "are not evildoers, but good people who come from good families"—they come "just one time a year to ask for charity" and to invite their host to the evening gumbo.

Fourth, Tee Mamou and Basile prize the homemade mask. Although the two communities differ significantly in their maskmaking and masking traditions, both evince great measures of creativity and innovation, featuring a greater percentage of screen masks than do most other Mardi Gras communities. These two communities rely upon a generally old-fashioned esthetic that favors what is homemade; even those who buy their masks are likely to buy from neighbors.

In contrast, at Mamou or Church Point, for example, screen masks are worn by few riders, perhaps one in twenty. The great majority wear store-bought, Halloween-style rubber or plastic masks, or half-face masks that cover only the nose and cheeks and a portion of the fore-head. A significant percentage wear only face paint. But in Basile, about half of the maskers wear screen-wire masks made in the community. And all of the Tee Mamou women wear either screen-wire masks or a needlepoint variety developed in the community. This book concentrates on the craftsmen of Basile and the craftswomen of Tee Mamou who make the masks most frequently worn in their respective communities.

What Happens on Mardi Gras Day

Most versions of the Cajun *courir de Mardi Gras* share a simple basic pattern, though there is substantial variation from place to place. Central to most country Mardi Gras enactments are the gathering of food, a communal meal, and a dance. The masked group known as the Mardi Gras performs the ceremonial function of begging for the food in a series of visits to neighbors' houses, where they obtain chickens, rice, green onions, and other ingredients for the gumbo to be shared later in the day. Having gathered the food, the maskers return to their point of origin and entertain spectators with dancing and parading. After a rest of two or three hours, they perform another processional dance to begin the evening *bal*. Then other, uncostumed couples join the Mardi Gras on the dance floor; the holiday ends on or before midnight, when the Cajun band has played its final song and the last dancer has left the floor.

2 3

Potic Rider leading Basile children in the Mardi Gras song, 1990.

Even before the dawn of Mardi Gras day, maskers begin arriving—singly or in small groups—at the site chosen for the group's departure; some are already masked, and they often play at hiding their identities from the others. Practicing certain sounds and gestures with each other, individual Mardi Gras create their roles: masks of sounds and actions to complement the material masks that they wear. As departure time nears, the group is addressed by a leader—in Tee Mamou, by Gerald Frugé, the *capitaine*; in Basile, by Potic Rider, president of the Mardi Gras Association—who will stand in command of the day's proceedings. The *capitaines*, co-*capitaines*, and other leaders go through the day unmasked; it is their job to mediate between the wild Mardi Gras and the unmasked spectators, ensuring that the day's play will not boil over into violence or vandalism. Thus, even before the procession begins, the mask possesses two purposes: assisting the players in their roles and separating them from their leaders.

After being frisked for concealed weapons and alcohol, the maskers pile into wagons. One large, brightly painted trailor holds all the Tee Mamou women; the larger Basile group fills two wagons, one for the men and one for the women. Led by a truck carrying the *capitaine*, and accompanied by other trucks carrying musicians and beer, the masked band begins its journey.

With the first stop, the group begins a pattern of ceremonial visitation that will be repeated twenty to forty times before the day ends. The *capitaine* stops his truck. As the Mardi Gras wait in their wagon, he walks alone into a neighbor's yard and asks the owner's permission for the Mardi Gras to visit. When consent is granted, the leader signals the Mardi Gras into the yard, where they sing their traditional song in French. Then, the musicians—now also in the yard—play a waltz and a two-step, begging dances performed to extract food or money from the host; it is important to "put on a show" good enough to earn the gifts that the Mardi Gras seek. After the song and dances, the farmer presents something to the *capitaine*—food for the gumbo or money for the beggars. The most sought-after reward is a live chicken.

Tee Mamou, 1992. *Capitaine* Gerald Frugé talks to the unmasked Mardi Gras and reporters before the group sets out.

2 5

Tee Mamou Mardi Gras
dance for their hosts as
musicians play, 1993.

Above:
At the evening *bal*, as well as at indoor stops during the day, Basile Mardi Gras dance in double-file lines; Da Office bar, 1996. Guiser on right wears plastic mask shaped similarly to the screen-wire masks sold in stores in the 1930s.

Left:
Mardi Gras Helena Putnam celebrates the capture of a chicken. Basile, 1993.

Left, above:
Between stops, on rest breaks, the Tee Mamou women often unmask, 1995.

Left, below:
Tee Mamou women take a break, 1992.

The Basile Mardi Gras
returns to town with a
parade down Main
Street, 1992.

If the host gives a chicken, a second ceremony of providing begins: the *capitaine* or the host throws the chicken into the air and the Mardi Gras run after it. The one who catches it is hailed as a victor, and the entire troupe celebrates the capture with free-form carousing until the *capitaine* summons them back to the road.

Captured chickens are placed in a cage in the captain's pick-up truck. In earlier times, chickens captured on Mardi Gras were eaten in that evening's gumbo. Today, however, the gumbo is made with prepurchased chickens; those captured during the day will be sold by the Mardi Gras Association or cooked at a later association event.

Throughout the day the Mardi Gras intermingle with, dance with, play tricks on spectators. In such tangled encounters, the mask, *capuchon*, and two-piece suit effectively mark the Mardi Gras apart from their audience. When visiting a house or in public procession between houses, all Mardi Gras are expected to keep their masks on. During long rides in isolated areas between house visits, or when drinking or eating along the route, however, they often remove their masks. Generally, revelers share their personal identities with each other while concealing themselves from outsiders.

More than any other part of Mardi Gras apparel, the mask separates the Mardi Gras from the spectator. This fact is most apparent on those extremely rare occasions when a participant carries Mardi Gras beyond its playful role with actions that threaten violence or vandalism. As an ultimate punishment, the *capitaine* demands that he or she remove the mask and walk home. Even wearing a two-pieced fringed suit, a Mardi Gras without a mask is no longer a Mardi Gras.

After a full day of house visits, the Mardi Gras has finished its run, at which time the *capitaine* leads the group in a parade back through the town. The whole town then shares a chicken gumbo and ends the evening with a community dance. Next morning is Ash Wednesday, day of atonement, beginning of Lent—and, as more than one rider has said, "If you do Mardi Gras right, you'll have enough to pray about when you get up early and go to church."

A Historical Sketch of the Screen Mask

There is no direct evidence to indicate the age and provenance of the Cajun Mardi Gras screen mask. Scraps of information, explored by Samuel Kinser, Georgie Manuel, and Ronnie Roshto, suggest that such masks came into fashion in the second half of the nineteenth century. First, in 1877 or slightly later, an Opelousas general store was apparently selling European-made, wire-screen masks made available from a wholesaler in New York. Second, also apparently in the late 1800s, screen masks were introduced into the John Canoe cele-

Oscar Miller wearing the *barbu* mask that he made with his stepfather, J. B. LeBlue, 1992.

Tee Mamou bearded
mask, 1995.

Tee Mamou bearded mask, 1991.

brations of the Caribbean, a region whose carnivals show several aspects of shared past traditions and likely mutual influence with rural Louisiana Mardi Gras.

Third, as screen wire was not invented until the 1860s, we can assume that such masks gained popularity shortly after they were introduced in Cajun country. The fact that the screen masks became prevalent within such a brief period of time in both Cajun and Caribbean celebrations suggests that they filled a vital practical purpose. The excellent ventilation afforded by screen wire would ensure its popularity, for Carnival in the Caribbean and even in Louisiana often takes place in very warm weather, which makes many riders avoid rubber masks and other types of facewear that are not well ventilated. Today in Basile, where screen wire is the preferred masking material, most people, when asked why they wear screen masks, will mention two major factors—comfort and tradition.

The earliest surviving record of country Mardi Gras maskers appears in a handwritten account from the late nineteenth century, which describes a group of *barbus* (bearded men) singing in "chorus." The term *barbu* suggests the fringe, made of animal hair or yarn, that dangles from the chins of many screen masks; even today, masks with such chin fringes are called *barbus*. Yet this information is so sketchy that we cannot determine if the bearded Mardi Gras were actually wearing screen masks.

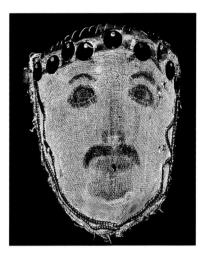

The oldest Cajun Mardi Gras screen mask yet identified, dating perhaps from c. 1910.

The earliest photographs reveal screen masks in astonishing numbers and variety. Photos shot in the 1930s, as well as surviving masks from earlier years, reveal that such maskmakers as Suson Launey, Vories Moreau, and Potic Rider currently craft masks that look very much like those made in Cajun country sixty to ninety years ago.

Residents of Basile and Tee Mamou who remember the masking traditions of the 1920s through the 1950s state that screen masks were the preferred facewear. Masks were sometimes handmade by the Mardi Gras themselves, but others were commercially produced and offered for sale in local stores. Some older Acadia Parish residents recall buying a preshaped screen form which they then painted; others bought masks that were prepainted as well. Hugh Miller, who ran Mardi Gras in

34

Above:
Tee Mamou mask with
characteristic long nose,
1994.

Left:
Kim Moreau of Basile
wearing a Mardi Gras
mask made in 1996 from
the heavy shellshaker
screen used in the oil
fields.

LeJeune Cove during the 1940s, recalls that "I never did run with a homemade mask. You could buy them there in the old mercantile in Iota. At that time they'd cost you ten or fifteen cents." Sometimes Mardi Gras "added some cloth on the inside" to make the mask less penetrable. Often they added other finishing touches such as a horsehair mustache or beard.

Masks worn in pre–World War II Basile were of two kinds. Vories Moreau, born in 1925, recalls that the wealthier Mardi Gras bought screen masks at the general store. In those times, the only screen masks worn in Basile were the store-bought kind: one-piece shells of screen cut in a scoop shape to fit the mask to the chin and pinched in the middle to accommodate the nose.

According to Vories, store-bought masks available in Basile in the 1930s were shaped with prominent chins and noses (much like the store-bought plastic masks of today) and decorated identically, with "blue eyes, red cheeks, and a black mustache." These masks, though popular, were not within the economic reach of all. Poorer residents continued a tradition of homemade denim masks, cut from scrap materials and sewn to cover the entire head, with the front pulled tight under the chin to fit the face closely. Eyeholes were cut in the denim, and women sewed on decorative touches, such as beards, eyebrows and mustaches made from horsehair or yarn, yarn tears and other facial orna-

mentation, or sometimes a nose protruding from the face. Vories Moreau remembers one young man who ran in the 1930s with a corncob nose sewn to his denim mask.

Some Acadia Parish residents remember masks made of cheesecloth worn by Mardi Gras in the 1960s. The fabric was dipped in flour-and-water paste to stiffen it, then draped over the wearer's face and allowed to dry before it was painted.

As recently as twenty years ago, according to Vories Moreau and others, the masks of Basile and Tee Mamou, as well as those of most other Mardi Gras communities, were all very much alike. The most notable variation occurred in terms of sewn additions to the screen—while most Basile maskmakers used paint exclusively to decorate the facial area of the masks, Tee Mamou maskmakers more often sewed on noses, eyebrows and other facial features to add a further decorative dimension. Maskmakers would "raid everything they could find to decorate it . . . anything that they thought would look good," one says. Cotton, wool, seedpods or "gumballs," twigs, squirrel tails, bones and twigs, chicken and guinea feathers were all used to make masks as "ugly" as possible. Masks in Tee Mamou and nearby communities like LeJeune Cove, Egan, and Iota often featured prominent noses. Some fabric noses hung limp and floppy, "like a bell's clapper," recalls Larry Miller of Iota.

As life changed, so did the materials commonly used for masks. Some mask-makers started using materials from the oil fields they worked in, like the shell-shaker screen preferred by Potic Rider and Kim and Vories Moreau of Basile, or a silicone glue compound favored by one or two Tee Mamou maskmakers for forming noses. Today, a number of local maskmakers use a lighter-weight nylon screen rather than (or in addition to) the heavier window screening.

Maskmaking Today

Today, many maskmaking specialists, including most featured in this book, fashion masks all year round. For most Cajuns, however, maskmaking begins some time after New Year's Day, as the community begins to build its Mardi Gras mood. Throughout January in Tee Mamou and Basile, there is much anticipatory talk in bars, stores, and homes. Both towns possess Mardi Gras associations that hold their first annual meeting in early January to make plans and to get the participants pumped up for the festival. At Tee Mamou, it is required that all participants memorize their Mardi Gras song before the celebration; much time at meetings is spent practicing this song.

As the Mardi Gras associations begin planning, maskmakers begin their work quietly at home. The craft is associated so intimately with the season that few people make masks except during the January and February days leading up to Mardi Gras. "It wouldn't feel right to make a mask any other time," said J. B. LeBlue of Basile. Thus maskmaking not only provides needed apparel for the *courir*, but also helps build the mood of anticipation.

Many people run Mardi Gras only once or twice, and then decide that the game is not for them; some of these nonpartici-pants will join the older people and children who follow the procession in cars or wait at one of the houses for the Mardi Gras to visit. But the backbone of Mardi Gras are the seasoned players who have run for many years—for them, Mardi Gras "is bigger than Christmas," an expression of almost proverbial currency often heard as the special day approaches. Among the revelers who "live for Mardi Gras" (another frequent expression) there are few who have not, at one time or another, made a Mardi Gras mask.

On any given year, however, there are probably no more than fifteen maskmakers at work in Basile. Although—counting the men, women and children together—there may be as many as two hundred faces needing masks, most don masks that they or their neighbors have made in preceding years. Others buy masks in stores or rely upon a community specialist to make them. In Basile, J. B. LeBlue and his family have crafted as many as forty masks in the

Above:
"The uglier it is, the better": Tee Mamou mask incorporating silicone glue.

Left:
Mardi Gras masks made by J. B. Le Blue of Basile during the 1996 and earlier Mardi Gras seasons.

weeks preceding Mardi Gras, loaning out or selling all but a few.

In Tee Mamou, a higher proportion of male and female Mardi Gras make their own masks, or buy a blank screen mask from a local maskmaker and decorate it themselves. Many prefer to make this—the single most expressive element of their disguise—themselves.

Historically, men have been the principal makers of Mardi Gras screen masks; as a rule, men and boys (usually the Mardi Gras themselves) have cut, shaped, and decorated the masks, although women often sew on the cloth or elastic borders. As women have begun running Mardi Gras, however, they have also begun making masks.

Some riders lavish days on planning and making their costumes. Others wait until the day before and then hastily throw together a suit, making or borrowing a mask at the last minute.

Cajuns craft two kinds of Mardi Gras masks: those worn throughout the day of house visits and those worn only for the processional and *bal* that end the festivities. In Basile, *bal* masks can be extremely varied and artful, but those to be worn during the day-long *courir* are designed with practical considerations foremost in mind. In Tee Mamou, however, the Mardi Gras perform demanding and often dangerous stunts at the dance. Although *bal* masks are often

fancier than those worn during the day, they must be comfortable as well as striking.

Today's maskmakers vary greatly in their approaches to the craft, but they share two important traits. First, continuing the tradition of their parents, they are very thrifty with the materials they use, continually conserving and recycling mask materials. Masks are often made entirely from household scraps hoarded throughout the year. And a good mask will itself be recycled from year to year, reappearing in many different forms; it may even be handed down from generation to generation.

Second, though conservation-conscious in their use of materials and tenacious in continuing to wear their best early crea-

Mardi Gras masks made by J. B. LeBlue of Basile in 1996.

39

tions, all have shown great creativity in incorporating new materials and techniques into the maskmaking process. As we have seen, some maskmakers have introduced materials from the oil fields where they worked, like the shellshaker screen preferred by some Basile craftsmen, or a silicone glue compound used by some Tee Mamou maskmakers for decoration.

Combining the newest techniques, the oldest designs, and a constant impulse to shock, the maskmakers of Tee Mamou and Basile create startling, sometimes confusing images: Suson Launey of Tee Mamou says that her guiding principle is "The uglier it is, the better it is." J. B. LeBlue of Basile may make a mask "so ugly that it's beautiful, or so beautiful that it's ugly." Beautiful, ugly, or both, the masks of Tee Mamou and Basile are striking and sometimes unforgettable creations.

MARDI GRAS IN BASILE

The Men and Their Masks

Mardi Gras *bal*, 1992,
with Tony Johnson,
center, wearing mask he
made from rabbit fur and
cow's horns.

THIS TOWN of approximately eighteen hundred inhabitants has celebrated Mardi Gras for as long as any of its citizens can remember. Before World War II, when the population of Basile was much smaller than it is today, and the outlying country more populous, separate all-male Mardi Gras runs visited the farms to the north and south of town. During the war, due at least in part to the fact that so many of the young men who formed the core of the festival were in uniform and far from home, Basile suspended its Mardi Gras. In the years following, before the Basile run was revived, some Basile men took part in other runs: for example, Vories Moreau ran in neighboring Tee Mamou. In the 1960s, the Basile run was revived, and it has taken place every Mardi Gras since that time.

The Basile run of recent years differs greatly from earlier enactments in at least three major ways. First, as the countryside has grown less populous and most of the former farmers have moved into town, the Basile Mardi Gras has spent more and more time in the midst of town. Instead of chasing chickens through pastures, as their fathers did, the young men and women of Basile often pursue the feathered prey over paved streets and trap them under cars. Second, the more urbanized landscape of Basile is one of the reasons why the Mardi Gras now travels on trucks instead of horseback. Third, since the early 1980s,

both men and women have run together on Mardi Gras day in Basile.

Basile Maskmakers
Vories and Kim Moreau represent the oldest continuous tradition of screen maskmaking in Basile; Potic Rider and the LeBlue family have made most of the screen masks now in use in Basile's Mardi Gras celebrations. There are two principal ways of learning maskmaking in Basile—

The oldest active mask in Basile. Vories Moreau's first Mardi Gras mask, worn by father, son and grandson continually since Vories made it in 1950; worn by Kim Moreau, 1996.

43

Kim Moreau, 1992, wearing the mask that his father Vories made in 1950 and performing the role of beggar, using a tin pail and traditional family begging gestures.

family tradition and independent invention. Kim Moreau, Potic Rider, and Oscar Miller learned by watching older relatives, their fathers and uncles. Vories Moreau and J. B. LeBlue, whose parents were not maskmakers, taught themselves simply by looking at masks and figuring out how to make them. We have been able to locate only a few instances of apprenticeship outside the family—only occasionally will an aspiring maskmaker has gone to Vories, for example, and asked to learn the craft.

Vories Moreau, who first ran Mardi Gras in 1933 at the age of seven, is one of Basile's most ardent Mardi Gras. After running more than twenty-five years, he became a *capitaine* in 1961; in 1995, he was named the first living member of Basile's Mardi Gras Hall of Fame. Vories's commitment to Mardi Gras has always been unshakable and nonnegotiable. Every employer he met in his youth got the same speech from Vories: "I'll work for you Christmas. I'll work for you Sunday. I'll work overtime every day. But I won't work on Mardi Gras. That's my day."

Vories was a member of Basile's Mardi Gras until it ceased running during World War II. In 1950, when Basile's celebration was still dormant, Vories was running again at neighboring Tee Mamou, where his wife's family lived. He wanted a screen mask, but the masks available in stores before the war were no longer found there.

So he acquired some heavy screen wire from the oil fields and began making his own—in a process similar to Potic Rider's, described below—using only his bare hands to give the mask a general shape and a broomstick to shape the nose and chin.

The mask that Vories Moreau made in 1950 can still be seen on Mardi Gras in Basile. Vories wore it for ten years before retiring from running; his son Kim has since worn the same mask for more than twenty consecutive Mardi Gras, and, for three years, Kim's son Brandon wore it to the Basile children's Mardi Gras on Sunday. Grandfather, son, and grandson have thus shared the same mask for nearly fifty years.

Vories's masks, made from the stiffest oil field screen available, are noted for their pleated chins, shaped by the rounded

Vories Moreau and Mike Broussard celebrating the Mardi Gras return to Basile, 1992.

45

end of a broomstick. Vories made about eight masks and passed on the tradition to his son Kim.

Potic Rider has run Mardi Gras every year since 1952, when he was seven. Currently president of Basile's Mardi Gras Association, Potic is also the lead singer of Basile's traditional Mardi Gras song. Making masks is simply part of Potic's complete commitment to the festival. He learned to make masks from his father and uncle. He made his first mask in 1955 or 1956—at age ten or eleven—and since then has made one hundred or more masks, eight of which he still owns; the others he gave to family members, friends, and to anyone in need of a mask on Mardi Gras. More than forty years later, his maskmaking techniques have changed little, although some of the materials have.

For Potic, no matter how beautiful the mask, practicality and comfort come first: "You're going to have that mask on all day. If you're going to chase chickens, you have to see—real well. If you're going to have that thing pressed up against your face for eight hours, it better be comfortable."

For all their practical qualities, Potic's masks are also visually striking. Among their most memorable features is their near transparency. Because Potic employs wide-mesh screen, the outline of the wearer's face is easy to see. In order to assure disguise, Potic is very careful in placing and coloring facial features on the screen: strategic designs on the mask's surface distort the wearer's features sufficiently to conceal his or her identity.

It takes about three and a half hours for Potic to make a mask. Except for the elastic border, sewn on by his wife, Sandy, he makes the entire mask.

Like his father and uncle before him, Potic begins by measuring the face vertically, from the center of the forehead to just below the chin, and horizontally, from midtemple to midtemple. A typical measurement is ten inches by eight inches; the mask is always a little wider than it is long. Potic uses the measurements as his guide in cutting a shield-shaped cardboard form which will serve as a pattern. Laying a piece of screen wire tight against the cardboard, Potic uses tinsnips to cut the screen. Careful trimming is essential, because loose wire could cut the face of the wearer during the physically taxing activities of Mardi Gras.

Although Potic made his first masks from window screen, he, like Vories Moreau, prefers the stiffer, more durable material called shellshaker screen, used in the oil fields for sifting gravel out of pipelines. For the past twenty years, all of Potic's masks have been made from shellshaker material.

Potic uses only his hands to shape the mask. His ideal mask is contoured to the face but touches it at only one point: the elastic-bordered top of the mask will

Above:
Potic Rider mask.

Left:
Potic designs the facial features of his masks to fit the face exactly. When the mask is worn off center, as in this photo [left], many otherwise obscure facial features are more easily seen; Potic's son, Russell Rider, Jr., left, and Kim Moreau in his father Vories's mask, 1996.

47

Waiting to invade a bar
for a pre–Mardi Gras
dance, 1996: Cassie
LeBlue, left, in J. B.
LeBlue's "bug-eye" mask,
shaped to accommodate
her eyeglasses; Shane
Lavergne, right,
in Potic Rider mask.

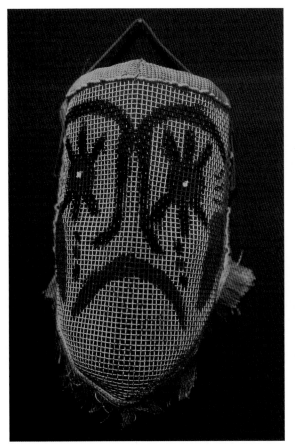

Potic Rider masks.

49

lie against the middle of the wearer's forehead. Although the form Potic uses is flat, the finished mask will have a convex shape. Potic first bends the cut wire along a vertical axis, with the nose at the peak, as if he were going to fold the mask in half; from the nose to the temple, the mask billows out about three inches from plane. Sometimes Potic further shapes the chin area by bending the wire at the bottom of the mask to fit the shape of the chin.

Potic usually begins decorating by spray-painting a black or white base coat on the screen. "White is the best, because it brings out all the other colors—especially red. But black is good, too—those are the two colors I always use." Only rarely does Potic paint eyes, nose, and mouth on the bare screen; sometimes, he puts a basecoat on one side of the mask and leaves the other half unpainted.

After the base paint dries, Potic holds the mask to his face and uses a pencil to mark the center of his eyes, so that he will paint the mask's eyes in the right place. With only two pencil marks as his guides, Potic then uses paint or Magic Marker to color in the facial features—eyebrows, eyes, nose, and mouth. His designs are basically traditional, influenced by the kinds of features that his father and uncles once had sewn on their denim masks. Most of his masks, like theirs, feature streaks on the cheeks (which Potic interprets as lines

of age and wisdom), eyes that stream tears, and a menacing frown.

About eleven years ago, Potic developed a distinctive design variation. He created a mask that was half-smiling and half-frowning, and he gave it a unique interpretation: "The frown stands for the Mardi Gras while they're begging, when they don't have enough food to feed the town. The smile is for the Mardi Gras at the end of the day, when they have all the food they need for the gumbo".

Bordering serves both to protect the wearer from the sharp points of cut wire and to enhance the decorative value of the mask and its function of concealment. This final stage is performed by Potic's wife, Sandy, who sews on the elastic border. Most of the older masks, including Potic's first efforts, had cloth borders, but "they didn't stand up well with all that wear and tear and sweat," and they had to be replaced every year. Elastic, on the other hand, will last for many years without tearing, and it is more effective than cloth for protecting the face from the sharp wire edges.

J. B. LeBlue was born in 1959 and has lived in Basile all but one year of his life. He has participated in Basile's Cajun Mardi Gras since he was ten, as a runner, wagon driver, and maskmaker. J. B. has so excelled in his craft that many other members of

Potic Rider bending shellshaker screen to shape a Mardi Gras mask, January 1996.

the community ask him and his family to provide their masks. To J. B., screen masks define Mardi Gras: "If you wear a rubber mask, that's Halloween, not Mardi Gras. If you wear face paint, that's Halloween. Screen masks are Mardi Gras—and only Mardi Gras."

J. B. is currently the most prolific mask-maker in Basile—in 1993 he made nearly forty masks, in 1996 thirty. Unlike Basile's other maskmakers, J. B. adopts an assembly-line method, making many masks at once. "It takes me five days to make one mask right," says J. B. "But I can make fifteen in the same amount of time, so that's what I do." J. B. is also unique among current Basile maskmakers in the degree to which he involves other family members in the process: as many as four people—J. B., his wife, Cassie, and two of their children—may work together on a single mask.

Even before the screen is cut, J. B. and his children create their designs. Laura, born in 1981, has been designing masks since she was seven; Jennie, born in 1990, began contributing her own designs at age four or five. The girls draw mask designs on ruled paper. J. B. may use elements of three or four different designs in his mask; he never copies the designs exactly, but always adds his own innovations.

With his children still at work on designs, J. B. begins cutting the screen wire. Unlike Vories, Kim, and Potic, who use the heavy shellshaker screen, J. B. prefers lighter screen, which he collects from discarded windows. The pliability of this softer wire allows J. B. to shape the mask more easily and to mold more facial details than he otherwise would.

J. B. lays the screen against a cardboard mold and cuts a rectangular or shield-shaped piece of wire with regular

51

J. B. mask with lines running down from eyes. One of his earliest masks, awaiting a new border, 1996.

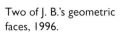
Two of J. B.'s geometric
faces, 1996.

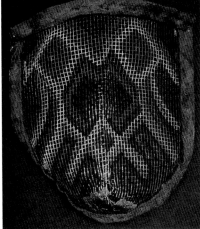

Above:
J. B. LeBlue, holding up the mask and suit made by him and his family for his daughter Jenny's first Mardi Gras in 1990.

Left:
One of J. B. LeBlue's earliest masks.

scissors. He uses three methods of crafting the chin area. The simplest is to make a straight bottom border without contours; most often, however, he bends the wire by hand to scoop out the chin area. His third method is to cut a vertical slit up the middle of the bottom border and gather the wire on either side of the slit into an overlapping triangle, creating a deep, pointed chin.

In some of his masks, J. B. creates raised areas for the eyes. He lays the screen over the plastic top of a large toothpaste dispenser and then bears down on the screen with a one-and-a-half-inch plumber's nut to mold the screen from both sides, creating a bug-eyed effect. J. B. first employed this technique in an effort to make maskwearing easier for those who wear glasses.

Another of J. B.'s innovations is what he calls the "beer drinker's special," which contains a hole for the mouth that allows wearers to eat and drink without pulling up their masks.

All of J. B.'s masks receive a base coat. Unlike Potic, J. B. seldom uses white, preferring green, red, and other bright colors. Once he has cut the screen and applied the base coat, J. B. uses a glue gun to hot-glue the borders of the masks, this being the most effective process he has found for covering the ends of wire that would otherwise protrude from the edges and cut the wearer. After the glue has dried, decoration begins. J. B. uses enamel paints, brushing freehand to render the designs that he adapts from his daughters'. These designs vary enormously, from skulllike shape and features, to highly geometric ornamentation.

To many of his masks, J. B. adds sequins and yarn. Like Potic's painted and drawn designs, J. B.'s yarn and sequin patterns feature lines running down the mask, but J. B. does not interpret these as reflecting old age and wisdom; instead, they represent a supernatural, almost divine look. J. B. favors startling and often complex designs. "I make them so ugly that they're pretty—or so pretty that they're ugly," he says, adding that many of his masks have been worn by the winners of Mardi Gras trophies in three different categories: Prettiest , Ugliest, and Most Original Mardi Gras.

In the final step, Cassie LeBlue, J. B.'s wife, sews on the borders. She irons strips of felt or patterned cloth and folds them over the mask's edges, and then uses fishing line—more durable than the thread J. B. once used, and almost invisible—to attach the border to the screen.

J. B.'s stepson Oscar has often worked on masks with J. B. and lately has been making his own. J. B. and Oscar together made Oscar's favorite mask—a unique creation with a base coat of white paint so thick that it closes in the holes in the screen wire; one can see through this mask only in the crucial area of the eyes. This mask is a *barbu*, covered with black, hairlike material all around the border. Oscar has caught dozens of chickens with this mask, which he was wearing in 1993 and 1994, both years when he was chosen by the Mardi Gras *capitaines* as the Best All-Around Male Mardi Gras.

Oscar has made both screen masks like his stepfather's and the more elaborate *bal* masks. He created his 1995 *bal* mask from a goat skull, which he painted and equipped with flashing lights lodged in the eye sockets.

Basile Masks in Action

The most important facet of the mask may be unseen—the freedom that it grants to create a new identity. At least as important as the colors and designs of the Mardi Gras mask is the dramatic way in which the wearer brings it to life. In terms of drama, the mask is both focal and diversionary—sometimes the wearer plays a role specifically geared to fit the mask he or she is wearing, but just as often the mask is simply an opportunity, providing the freedom and anonymity that allows the wearer to adopt the role that he or she would be playing under any mask on Mardi Gras day.

Each Cajun town's Mardi Gras plays many overlapping roles, including *sauvage*, outlaw, beggar, thief, and fool. Every celebration will engage all of these roles to some extent, yet each group creates its own identity by elevating some above the others. At Basile, *sauvage* and beggar constitute perhaps the two most prominent roles.

In Basile all of the maskers are called *sauvages*—or "savages"—the Cajun word for "Indians." Basile's *sauvages* do not resemble mainstream America's stereotypes of Indians (e.g., no one wears buckskin or warpaint), but they shape themselves to a traditional Cajun image of the Indian role. The old-style Mardi Gras costumes, made largely of burlap feed sacks, featured fringes along the arms and legs; the fringe was interpreted as Indian dress by people who ran Mardi Gras before World War II. Today's costumes are more elaborate, but the fringe remains.

Younger Basile maskers do not see themselves as Indians in quite the same way as their parents and grandparents did. Most people under forty will say that Mardi Gras are called *sauvages* because both Mardi Gras and Indians are wild, but the younger people do not see their costumes or masks as imitating Indian dress or face paint.

Today's *sauvage* is an invader of public space who breaks away from the Mardi Gras procession to stop cars, creep up on and abduct children, and carry off photographers. Their mock terrorism tests the boundaries of playfulness. The *sauvages* not only embody toughness, but also project a real sense of menace, which is represented, to some extent, by the frowns that prevail on the Basile masks.

56

Mardi Gras gesturing
from the men's wagon as
they ride through town,
1992.

Basile men in their Mardi Gras wagon, trying on their masks and roles before setting out, 1992. The two masks in the foreground were made by Potic Rider.

One of Potic Rider's half-frowning, half-smiling masks, representing the two moods of the Mardi Gras. Worn by Shane Lavergne as he scales a telephone pole, 1993.

Far left:
"Stealthy and conspicuous at the same time": Basile Mardi Gras crouches in the road with a chicken he has just taken, 1992.

Left, above:
Two Basile Mardi Gras creep into Betty's Bearcat Lounge, 1992.

Left, below:
Mardi Gras *sauvage* antics. Basile Mardi Gras hoists photographer Helena Putnam into the air and holds her over a fire ant hill, 1992.

61

Piling off the wagon, *sauvages* steal forward, crouching and lurching, emitting high-pitched whoops, trying to look both conspicuous and stealthy at the same time. It is a funny and disconcerting combination. Part of the *sauvage* role is to turn menace into laughter by putting on a stunning show with slapstick gestures and insane behavior. One of the most impressive acts of playfulness in Basile is climbing; athletic Mardi Gras scale roofs, trees, and telephone poles as the *capitaines* try to whip them back to earth.

Both Vories Moreau and Potic Rider were excellent Mardi Gras *sauvages*. They distorted their voices and movements so effectively that they could dance with their own wives and mothers and remain undetected. But both Vories and Potic were such consummate tricksters that they would eventually reveal themselves through the outrageousness of their tricks. Here is Vories's account of one of the tricks he performed in the 1950s:

> We went to one house—they had a lot of chickens. And they threw out a chicken, and we caught it and we started playing around. The woman was looking kind of suspicious, like maybe we were going to get some more chickens out of their yard. So I went behind the barn out of sight, out in the field. And I picked up this big, dry cow patty, and I stuck it under my suit, you know.

I started walking back toward the road, looking like I had something to hide. That old woman called me: "Come back here, Mardi Gras—I know you've got my chicken." I made like I was going to run, and the *capitaine* came and whipped me back to the porch. I was clutching the side of my suit. The old woman said, "Okay, Mardi Gras, show me what you got."

I got on my knees and bowed my head down. Then I pulled out that cow patty and laid it right at her feet. She started yelling, "Vories, *maudit!* Get out of my yard!"

Mardi Gras Syd Fontenot begs for coins in the Woodman Hall. Basile, 1992.

Vories's tricks were so much a part of his Mardi Gras identity that they allowed his neighbors to see through his costume.

The beggar role appears in all Mardi Gras, particularly as the maskers dance and sing for a chicken. In Basile, however, begging assumes a more pronounced role, one at least as important as chasing chickens. Here, not just the farmer, but every passerby is fair game. A Mardi Gras will approach you on his knees, with one palm extended and a finger from his other hand pointing into the empty palm. "*Tit cinq sous*" ("five little pennies"), the masked men say, in their high-pitched "Indian" voices. This groveling game may at first

62

Growing a bit more pushy, two Basile Mardi Gras crowd the photographer to beg, 1992.

seem a pure pitch for charity, but there is a strong undercurrent of extortion that can surge into intimidation as the beggar, pretending to shine your shoes for pennies, will unlace them instead, then unbuckle and strip off your belt, and remove your hat. Thus the beggar and *sauvage* roles often mesh.

For Potic Rider, begging is essential to both the origin and the nature of Cajun Mardi Gras. He explains the purpose of the Mardi Gras house visits: "You're not doing this for you, now. The Mardi Gras's not doing this for them, now. It's for the town. So they can eat one last good meal before Lent starts. *That's what it's all about.*"

In Potic's theory about how Mardi Gras

originated, begging plays the central role: "Mardi Gras started in France when the people didn't have enough to eat. They went to their neighbors to beg for food, and they wore masks so their neighbors wouldn't know who they were."

For Vories Moreau, so skillful at playing the *sauvage*, good begging was just as important as any other part of Mardi Gras. Vories would go to great lengths to secure Mardi Gras food:

The Mardi Gras always asks for more than what it gets—and they get as much as they can. I'd kneel down and I'd kiss their hand and I'd shine their shoes and I'd kiss their feet, and if they'd give me

63

a chicken I'd want the rice, and if they give me the rice I'd want the grease [lard]. If they give me the grease, I want the roux. . . . I'd never give up. I always wanted something else, you know.

I'd sing and I'd ask them, I'd tell them, "Look, the Mardi Gras didn't get no chickens today." And I was lying, but I'd tell them that, you see. I'd say, "We didn't get no chickens." And they'd tell me, "Well, we're going to give you some rice." And I'd say, "Well, we have plenty of rice, but nobody gives us a chicken."

Today in Basile, begging remains a polished art. Vories's son Kim Moreau, who carries a tin pail and a sign with him on his procession, is noted as an exceptional beggar. One of his exploits—sliding the diamond ring off the finger of a woman as she was dropping money in his pail—is often retold.

Three Basile Mardi Gras overwhelm a spectator who hasn't yet contributed enough, 1992.

The Basile Bal

By the time the gumbo is served at Basile—about four in the afternoon—a Mardi Gras may have performed as many as eighty dances, thirty chicken chases, a number of exhausting feats such as climbing, and a long processional dance through the center of town. In the three hours separating the gumbo from the beginning of the *bal*, the stress of the day has time to show itself—older Mardi Gras find their legs stiffening up, and even the younger ones have to catch a second wind before their final performance. Yet most will steel themselves for the processional entrance that begins the Mardi Gras *bal*—the most prolonged and spectacular single performance of the day. By seven most of the spectators are already at the dance hall, visiting and drinking while the Mardi Gras waits outside, often playing the game of straining to break into the hall, pushing at

64

Bal processional: dancing double file, the Basile Mardi Gras enters the Woodman Hall, 1993.

the hall door which is held shut by one of the *capitaines*. Finally, when the band strikes up the Mardi Gras song, the *capitaine* leads the group into the hall, and they dance forward in double file, forming a long line of swaying bodies. The dancers weave up and down, alternately dropping into a crouch and rising as they trace a wide circular path through the dance hall.

Now that no more chicken chases will occur, many of the Mardi Gras wear a second, more elaborate and less durable, costume for the *bal*. Masking assumes a broader range of possibilities. In Basile, Tony Johnson, one of the Mardi Gras's most active screen maskmakers, has created some of the wildest *bal* costumes, including a mask made from a cow's pelvis, a rabbit's fur costume, and a "dead man," with a black robe, white face paint, and a

65

noose dangling from his neck. "I find my costumes in the woods," Tony says, referring to the bones and fur that he works so artfully into his disguises.

After the grand processional, the men and women perform separate processions and dances, as judges decide who should be awarded the titles of Prettiest, Ugliest, and Most Original Costume, and the *capitaines* announce their decision of which man and which woman was Best All-Around Mardi Gras. After this half-hour or so of sustained performance, Mardi Gras linger to dance, drink, and narrate their holiday exploits for as long as their endurance permits. By midnight, most have left, but those who remain have been in continuous play-action for eighteen hours or more. The music and drinking will stop at midnight, as Ash Wednesday begins. Many will be in church at seven the next morning; some of the Mardi Gras, like Potic Rider, will drink their last beer on Mardi Gras night and won't open another until after Easter Sunday. Their masks are off now, and the great majority will not make or wear a Mardi Gras mask for another ten or eleven months, until early next year.

Above:
Mardi Gras *bal*, 1992; Tony Johnson wears the mask he made from rabbit fur and cow's horns.

Below:
Oscar Miller's goat skull mask, made for the 1995 Basile Mardi Gras *bal*.

66

Tee Mamou Mardi Gras
holding a child.

THE RURAL NEIGHBORHOOD known as Tee Mamou ("Little Mamou") lies between two bayous in western Acadia Parish, in a landscape of crawfish ponds, rice and soybean fields, and scattered groups of homes. Tee Mamou has a long Mardi Gras tradition, having hosted a men's run for as long as anyone can remember. Residents say that it has taken place uninterrupted at least since the early 1900s, and probably longer.

More than two decades ago, several women whose families were active in the men's run founded their own run on the weekend before Fat Tuesday. Similar women's runs in nearby Basile and Eunice eventually merged with local men's *courirs*. But the Tee Mamou women's Saturday run, gumbo, and dance remain separate and vital, attracting twenty to fifty women and teenaged girls yearly. For many years, Gerald Frugé—assisted by senior cocaptain Claude Durio and several younger cocaptains—has been *capitaine* for both men and women, and all participants belong to the local Mardi Gras Association.

The women's and men's routes—planned during the weeks before Mardi Gras—cover largely different territory, however. The women's run takes place almost entirely in the countryside, and no longer ends with a parade through the town of Iota.

Running Mardi Gras remains a family tradition in Tee Mamou. Many longtime women Mardi Gras have daughters who began running as soon as they turned thirteen; their husbands, sons, or fathers participate in the men's run. Women often pass on their handmade masks and costumes to male relatives for their Tuesday run.

Many Tee Mamou women make their own masks, creating only one each year. But three local women—recognized as talented and prolific maskmakers—provide masks yearly for a number of participants.

Tee Mamou Maskmakers

Suson Launey, Renée Frugé, and Jackie Miller all began making masks for their own use or for their families. Now each creates no fewer than ten masks a year; Suson and Jackie, who also sell their masks at festivals and in shops, make dozens. All typically work on several masks at once and have developed an efficient assembly-line approach to many steps. They now work year round on maskmaking, but the heaviest volume is still just before Mardi Gras.

Although Tee Mamou masks vary widely in decoration, they share many similarities. Virtually all are constructed of either wire or plastic screen. Tee Mamou maskmakers favor pliable screen made of galvanized aluminum or nylon, which is easy to work with. Typically, about half of the women Mardi Gras wear screen-wire masks, and half wear needlepoint masks worked on lightweight plastic screen. An innovation

69

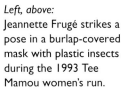

Left, above:
Jeannette Frugé strikes a pose in a burlap-covered mask with plastic insects during the 1993 Tee Mamou women's run.

Left, below:
Screen mask with fried egg eyes, 1994.

created by Suson Launey, needlepoint has been adopted by others as a more comfortable alternative to wire screen.

Maskmakers continue the local tradition of decorating their masks with whatever materials appeal to their imaginations: rubber insects, silk flowers, costume jewelry and Mardi Gras beads. Novelty items become part of their designs, as eyes are created from plastic fried eggs or a nose from a tiny chicken. Features are usually exaggerated and enlarged. A long, pointed nose is characteristic of Tee Mamou masks, as is abundant facial hair. Beards and mustaches are created with yarn, feathers, and strings of beads, and the traditional *barbu* sometimes becomes a mask entirely covered with hair.

Suson Launey and Renée Frugé are both active Mardi Gras who began making masks for their own use. Their designs appealed to other Mardi Gras, and their masks are now sought by many Tee Mamou women. Jackie Miller is an Iota-based maskmaker who does not run Mardi Gras, but started making masks when her sons joined a neighborhood children's run. Today, her masks are found less often than Suson's or Renée's in the women's run, but are popular in both the Tee Mamou men's and children's runs, and in several other *courirs*.

For the most part, these maskmakers have taught themselves rather than learning maskmaking directly from others. Suson Launey and Jackie Miller both developed their own methods and styles after closely observing other masks. As Suson says, "If you run Mardi Gras, you're going to see screen masks. . . . If I can see it, I can do it." Renée Frugé, a second-generation Mardi Gras, learned partly by watching her mother, Linda, and partly through independent invention. Like Suson and Jackie, she has devised techniques and designs that make her masks stand out.

All three women constantly search for innovative ideas and materials for their masks. They save and recycle the materials of everyday life: fabric scraps stuffed with quilt batting become noses, an old zipper becomes a mouth. They also regularly browse at discount stores and garage sales, looking for interesting materials and bargains. Renée Frugé searches out items that make her think, "Ah, that would look good, that's ugly, this is gross."

Suson Launey is a native of Iota, a town of fewer than thirteen hundred people situated just east of Tee Mamou. Iota has long been associated with the Tee Mamou *courir*—organizational meetings are held there, and both the men's and women's dances often take place there.

Suson has been making masks for more than seventeen years, since she started running Mardi Gras. Her daughter Crystal, now twenty, joined the women's run as soon as she was old enough.

When Suson first began running Mardi

Left, above:
Needlepoint masks worn during the 1990 run.

Far left, below:
Mask made by Suson Launey for the 1996 Tee Mamou women's Mardi Gras dance.

Left, below:
Suson Launey models her first screen-wire mask during the 1996 run.

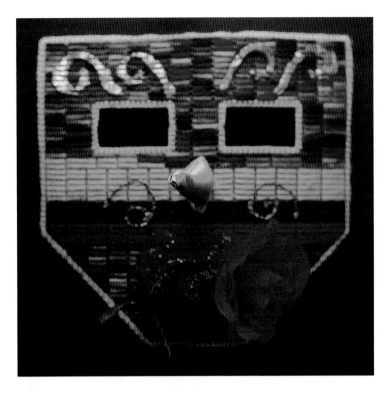

Needlepoint mask with contrasting bands of color, 1996.

Gras, some women wore screen masks, but others preferred homemade cloth masks because "a woman's face scratches easy," she says. Her earliest masks were made of wire screen, but she found that they gouged her face as she "cut up" and tangled with captains throughout the day. As a solution, she made a yarn mask stitched on soft plastic mesh rather than wire screen. This innovation "was something to hold true to the tradition of a screen mask but something to help prevent me from gouging up my face," Suson explains.

Almost immediately, other women began asking her to make needlepoint masks for them. Today, these masks are a hallmark of the Tee Mamou women's run. Many women continue to wear older examples of Suson's work for years; a few women (and at least one man) now create their own versions.

One of the needlepoint mask's main advantages is comfort. Although they are not as cool as wire masks, they are "so much more comfortable, especially if you're an active Mardi Gras," Launey says. She adds, "If you're going to cut up or intend to cut **73**

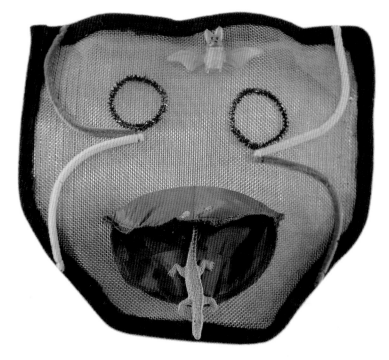

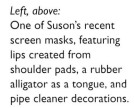

Left, above:
One of Suson's recent screen masks, featuring lips created from shoulder pads, a rubber alligator as a tongue, and pipe cleaner decorations.

Left, below:
Mask with glittery mouth cut out of fabric and glued onto needlepoint background.

74

up, you're going to *get* cut up" wearing a screen mask.

Suson still makes some wire screen masks and sometimes wears one herself. The kinds of masks she makes depend partly on what materials are available. Old-fashioned window screen is the best for wire masks, she says, but "you can't find that hard stiff screen anymore." Most of her wire masks are now made with the more pliable galvanized metal screen.

Suson starts with certain "ideas of what I want" in a mask but never sketches her designs in advance. Instead, she improvises as she goes, according to "whatever mood I'm in when I pick up the mask. That's the way it comes out." To make a needlepoint mask, she first cuts a tapered shield shape from a sheet of plastic screening, using an already-cut mask as a template. Her masks extend slightly above and below the face, and are usually as broad as they are long. Using the template, she then cuts rectangular holes in the mesh for the eyes. Correct placement of the eyeholes is essential, since the rest of the mask will be opaque.

Next, Suson stitches the entire mask. Using a tapestry needle threaded with four-ply yarn, she makes one basket-weave stitch for every four holes in the plastic screen; tighter needlework would make breathing through the mask difficult.

The yarn background provides the most basic decoration. Some masks are stitched from a single color of yarn. Others feature blocks of contrasting colors or rows of variegated yarn blending four colors. After a border is stitched around its edges, the mask is ready for decoration. Other than their needlework foundation, she says that her yarn masks are decorated "like any other mask" in the Tee Mamou run, using "anything and everything you can get ahold" of.

She first hot-glues a nose—usually made of colorful cloth stuffed with polyester filling—to the stitched background. Suson occasionally makes short, blunt noses, but more often they are long and pointed, frequently with hooked tips. Although long noses can also be seen on masks by other maskmakers in the area, Suson says that her particular fondness for them dates to an incident when she first started running Mardi Gras. One onlooker remarked that the Mardi Gras were always sticking their noses where they had no business, she says, and since then "I've been making my noses big enough to stick."

The noses also serve a practical purpose, providing a handle for pushing the mask away from the face or pulling it into place. Countless times throughout the day, the Mardi Gras unmask for beer stops or during long rides on the truck, lifting the mask up and to the side to rest on the *capuchon*.

Next, Suson creates an oversized mouth with cutouts of satin or felt or with

Suson estimating placement of eyes in plastic mesh (*top*) and stitching mask with basket weave stitch (*bottom*).

75

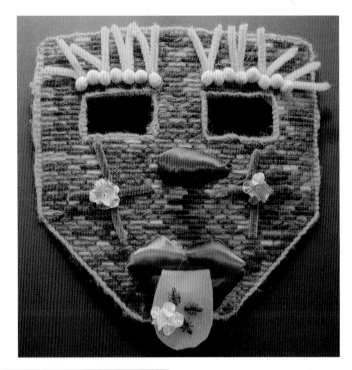

Left, above:
Needlepoint mask of variegated yarn with satin lips and felt tongue is an example of Suson Launey's current work.

Left, below:
Suson wore this mask during the 1996 run. The mouth, cut from a commercial rubber mask, was glued and sewn onto a flesh-colored needlepoint mask. Bangs are made of Spanish moss.

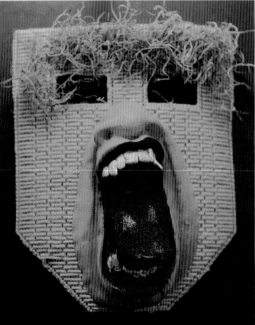

a pair of shoulder pads. Often she adds a protruding tongue or fangs. A gaping mouth and tongue, cut from a rubber Halloween mask, was the focal point of the needlepoint mask Suson wore in a recent run.

After gluing facial features in place, Suson sews them onto the mask. "If you don't sew everything down, the way Mardi Gras cut up there would be nothing left of the masks when the run is over," she says. She then adds other details: Mardi Gras beads, feathers, spirals of tinsel and colored pipe cleaners, rubber snakes and other creatures. The final step is sewing on a wide elastic strap to hold the mask in place.

Renée Frugé, a second-generation maskmaker, was born and raised in the Tee Mamou Mardi Gras tradition. Her father is *capitaine* Gerald Frugé, and her mother, Linda, has been a frequent participant in the women's *courir* since its early years. Renée's sister, Jeannette, usually runs with the women, and her two brothers act as cocaptains.

Renée "rode with [the Mardi Gras] forever" in the captain's truck before she began to run in 1989 at age thirteen. She has been making masks for most of that time, but her family has been involved in maskmaking far longer. Linda Frugé usually made her own masks, as did Renée's uncles.

Friends who admired Renée's work

soon began asking her to make masks for them. Now, she makes at least ten each year, giving away or selling most. She works on masks almost year round, "whenever I have a chance," and wherever she can find space. She recently bought a shed to use as a workshop. Some of Renée's ideas and techniques come from having observed Linda Frugé make masks over the years. But to a great extent she is a self-taught artist and has developed her own style through experimentation.

Like Suson, Renée begins with a general idea of what the mask will look like and then invents while working. Odd items discovered around the house or at discount stores (such as tire treads, feather dusters, and potholders) may spark an idea for a mask. She often uses her mother's old sewing materials for decoration as well.

Renée makes her masks from galvanized aluminum screen that she buys in rolls from hardware stores. Working freehand, she cuts a square from the roll. She may look at another mask to estimate shape and size, but typically "I just kind of judge it, like with cooking." She cuts the mask a little longer than her face, but "I don't like it too long to where [the wearer] can't look down."

She tapers the mask by trimming its lower edges. The scraps are saved to make "weird noses" and other features. The galvanized screen needs little further shaping to the face, but its cut ends must be care-

77

Screen mask made by
Renée Frugé and worn
in the 1994 run shows
her inventive use of
materials: potholder yarn
covers the mask, and a
bone pierces its nose.

Renée's favorite "mink" mask, which she has worn for several years in a row.

Hairy mask by Renée Frugé.

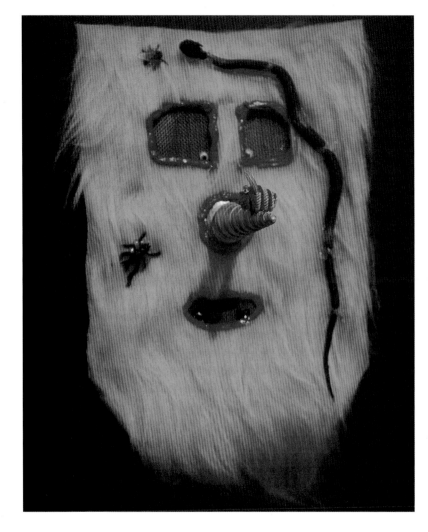

Above:
1996 screen mask by
Renée Frugé is covered
with raffia; a toy animal
forms the nose.

Left:
One of Renée's
animalistic screen masks
covered with fake fur and
decorated with a rubber
snake and insects.

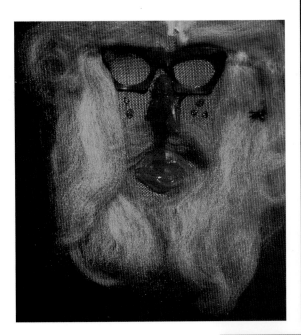

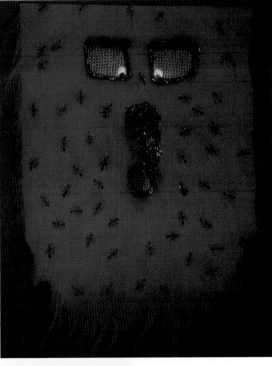

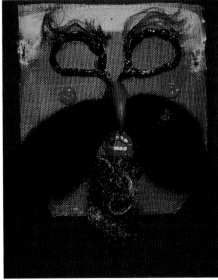

Above:
Screen mask with a nose and mouth created from hot glue. Irregularities and drips from the glue are purposely left to make the mask "uglier."

Above:
Renée's furry red, ant-covered mask has a warty nose made from blue silicone gasketmaker.

Left:
Screen mask by Renée Frugé, with eyes outlined with silicone basketmaker and "gag" teeth.

fully trimmed and bound to keep the wires from scratching the wearer's face. Renée has recently begun using hot glue to bind the cut edges. This not only prevents unravelling, but provides a transparent finish that eliminates the need for a decorative cloth border.

After binding, Renée begins decorating the mask with "whatever Mom has hanging around the house." A shaggy, wild appearance is especially characteristic of Renée's masks. She often covers masks with fake fur, fabric, raffia, or feathers. Renée's favorite creation, which she has worn for the last few years, is a "mink" mask with a pink pig's snout made from a thread spool and puff paint. She remarks that "I always made [my masks] kind of resemble an animal and I didn't know why, but I did. . . . I just like to do it to try to scare the kids."

Her opaque masks are popular with many Tee Mamou Mardi Gras who want to be so thoroughly disguised that only their eyes remain visible. Renée says, "I find that a lot of the masks I sell, [the Mardi Gras] like to be hidden behind it." However, she must also consider comfort, making sure that the wearer can both breathe and see well. Before she glues the fabric in place, she holds the mask against her face and looks in a mirror to determine where the eyes will be. She carefully marks the eyes with dents in the screen, or tacks down cutouts of felt with glue.

One of Renée's favorite materials is a colored silicone compound, which she uses to make noses and to outline eyes. This is one of the tricks she learned from her mother. Renée says, "I remember the . . . silicone because she'd made this big wart on my [mask's] nose. And I loved the way it felt—I thought it was so neat. So I looked all over" for silicone gasketmaker when she began making masks herself.

Renée also likes plastic "gag" features, which she buys from novelty stores or "wherever they have little ugly teeth or something." In a recent innovation, she has begun making her own noses and mouths from hot glue, using store-bought features as molds. Not only do these homemade features adhere to the masks better, but they allow more flexibility in decoration. To save time, she often makes several casts simultaneously. She then paints each with at least three coats of crafts paint. She does not trim the drips of glue that form on the noses or mouths, because they only make the masks "uglier".

Once the main features are in place,

Renée creates noses and mouths from hot glue, then paints them.

82

she adds other details, a process which often continues until she sells or gives away a mask. Renée says, "This is something else I do—I add later" as finishing touches occur to her. Her creations often become collaborative efforts as friends and relatives offer suggestions.

After Linda Frugé sews an elastic band onto the mask, it falls flat against the wearer's face. Renée and Linda check the mask for comfort, gluing strips of foam rubber onto the back to cushion pressure points. The mask will quickly become uncomfortable if "you've got wire rubbing on your nose all day long," Renée says. Later, she can adjust the mask to fit a particular Mardi Gras by bending the screen along the middle.

Jackie Miller, a native of Iota, vividly remembers the local men's Mardi Gras visiting her school each year during the 1950s and chasing the schoolgirls through the halls. She first became involved in the Mardi Gras tradition almost two decades ago when her young sons joined a family *courir* in nearby Egan. Jackie made masks for her sons and a few friends whose mothers "didn't want to fool with it." When her sons later joined Tee Mamou's men's run, she began making masks for other riders, too.

She now works year round to make about two hundred masks, she estimates; she sells many at festivals. Her masks

are worn by only a few of Tee Mamou's women, but are popular in the local men's and children's runs and with tourists.

Jackie has tried various kinds of screen over the years. Today she frequently binds two types together: metal screen on the outside because "it's shiny and holds its shape," and dark-colored plastic screen inside. This combination makes the mask less revealing and more comfortable, she says.

In decorating, she begins with the nose, eyes, and mouth because "to me, you have to have all your features." Many of Jackie's masks have downturned, drooping mouths: "I usually make mine sad. You always try to make the mask ugly. And sad is more ugly than happy." She adds, "If it's pretty, you're not afraid of it".

Next, she may add a beard and mus-

A variety of Jackie Miller's masks, many with sad, downturned mouths. She now makes at least two hundred masks a year.

tache, ears with pipe cleaner earrings, and other details. Like other Tee Mamou maskmakers, she shops all year for "ugly things on sale" to add to her masks.

All of her masks feature a bell pinned to the tip of the long, fabric nose. Jackie does not remember where she first got this idea, but she always adds a bell, because "it belongs there."

Tee Mamou Masks in Action

House visits in the countryside are often far apart, and, as their truck winds along narrow roads, Mardi Gras unmask to talk, drink and relax. When the procession stops at a home or business, the captain asks the owners for permission to visit. His request is largely a formality, as the hosts usually have agreed in advance to accept the Mardi Gras. But only after the captain signals their acceptance by blowing his whistle do the women dismount. As they pull masks into place, they are once more transformed into Mardi Gras.

Masking signals the beginning of their performance and frees the Mardi Gras to "cut up" and play the clown. Renée Frugé says, "When you put the mask on, it's so different. You can act the fool. And [onlookers] never know who it is." The Mardi Gras "can go behind someone they know, and stand right behind them . . . [and] look them straight in the eyes . . . and we can have a big smile on our face and they can't tell who we are. And they're sitting out there trying to figure it out."

Shirley Reed, wearing a screen mask featuring long eyelashes, with captain Claude Durio during a stop at a neighborhood store, 1992.

Tee Mamou Mardi Gras play much the same range of overlapping roles as those found in Basile—trickster, beggar, thief and outlaw, daredevil. Skilled Mardi Gras slip easily from one role to another. Although these traditionally male roles are now sometimes played by women, they are not specifically male or female. Masks may have beards or feminine-looking eyelashes—or both— but one masker explains that "we're just Mardi Gras".

Seasoned Mardi Gras begin performing as they climb from their truck and "take off at full steam," in Suson's words. They build excitement with high-pitched whoops as they link arms and form a column of two or four abreast. Singing their begging song loudly in unison, the Mardi Gras walk slowly towards the homeowners awaiting them in the front yard. Some "cut up" by crawling on hands and knees, or by pretending to read a newspaper as they approach.

As the maskers finish their song, uncostumed musicians begin a fast-paced two-

84

Left, above:
Tee Mamou Mardi
Gras approach a house,
singing their song in
unison. Several clown by
crawling on hands and
knees, 1993.

Left, below:
The two leading the Tee
Mamou procession "cut
up" by pretending to
read a newspaper as they
walk, 1993.

85

Renée Frugé pretends to fish from a stationary boat during a 1995 house visit.

step and then a waltz. Mardi Gras dance with each other or pull onlooking men, women and children into their dance. Some slink away from the crowd, circling toward nearby barns, sheds, and fields in search of opportunities to "pull some stuff there," one says. Like the Basile maskers, they are both surreptitious and conspicuous in their mischiefmaking, ensuring that the captains notice and pursue them.

Many of Tee Mamou's pranks and gestures are similar to those seen in other Cajun runs. Women climb porch supports or swing from trees. They improvise comedy around whatever they discover during their visit, riding children's bicycles, rolling spare tires, pretending to warm themselves over imaginary fires or to fish from a trail-

ered boat. They pantomime everyday activities that are made strange, and thus funny, by the maskers' appearance, as they sweep a driveway or act out a silent conversation with spectators.

Tee Mamou Mardi Gras announce themselves as beggars and supplicants; their song's final verse tells their hosts that "*on vous demande un peu de chose*" ("we ask you for a little something"). They expect donations in exchange for their "show"; traditional gifts include chickens or other gumbo ingredients. Although some homes offer live chickens or guineas for the women to chase, more often the host hands a frozen chicken or package of sausage to the captains.

Another traditional offering is money,

Tee Mamou Mardi Gras
climbs a tree while a
captain tries to get her
down, 1991.

Tee Mamou Mardi Gras
in a tree, 1996.

for which the Mardi Gras beg individually and en masse. Fingers pointing to cupped palms, they beseech onlookers for "*tit cinq sous*". Coins are tossed onto the ground, and Mardi Gras scramble to collect them and hand them to the captains.

Yet begging in Tee Mamou is rarely as persistent as it is in Basile. Playing the thief is perhaps more important. Tee Mamou women elevate their comic thefts to an art and to high comedy. They raid gardens, henhouses, and back yards to snatch green onions, eggs and chickens, spare tires or old clothes, and even children. Many women sew a roomy pocket to the front of their Mardi Gras suit to hold contraband like stolen chickens.

The range of available roles also includes that of daredevil. Some women dive through barbed wire and mud to catch chickens, ride pastured ponies or cows, and halt cars on the highway much as male Mardi Gras do. Others, though, focus more on clowning in ways they term "mischievous" and "witty" rather than emphasizing the physically daring.

Linda Frugé says of chasing chickens, "I never cared to do it, that wasn't my thing." Instead, "I always looked for a tire to roll or a bike to ride, or something that would entertain the kids, you know, and just do my little thing in that respect." A time-honored prank involves someone hiding by climbing into a barrel or ice bin, making sure that her mask's nose or *capuchon's* tip

remains visible. Today, Linda often finds that her daughters have beaten her to these tricks.

Still, play is often very physical: throughout the day, the maskers run, climb, and tumble. A particular feature of the Tee Mamou women's run is the constant mock battle waged between Mardi Gras and captains. The women "pick at" their male captains, teasing and playing tricks on them, and often tackling them and trying to wrest their whips away. Frequently, several women unite to overwhelm a captain, pinning him to the ground until other captains come to his rescue. In return, the Mardi Gras are chased and whipped. Such roughhousing is cooperative, and is understood by Mardi Gras, captains and onlookers alike as part of the entertainment. Suson Launey says, "It's to put on a show for the people, it's kind of like earning what they're going to give us."

But even as they play at fighting, theft and anarchy, women take care not to damage their hosts' property or frighten their children. They often unmask to reassure crying children, and engage youngsters in dances or games of pursuit. For many years, Tee Mamou women have offered children candy to allay their fears.

The *capitaine* signals the end of the visit

A Tee Mamou Mardi Gras holds a chicken she has captured, 1991.

88

by calling out, "All right, Mardi Gras, let's go!" However, the maskers make a game of refusing to depart. They grasp trees, lock arms and legs with each other, or try to outrun captains, who must herd or carry them back into the truck.

When the wagon returns to the Frugé barn late Saturday afternoon, the Mardi Gras have been singing, dancing, and "cutting up" for eight or nine hours. Suson Launey says that experienced Mardi Gras slow down in the afternoon after "running hard all morning." They are pacing themselves for the evening dance, which is for some Mardi Gras the day's most important performance.

At the barn, Mardi Gras and captains are served a meal of chicken-and-sausage gumbo and potato salad prepared by community members. Households and businesses that welcome the Mardi Gras during the day are in turn invited to the communal gumbo. Most, however, attend the dance instead. Yet this traditional sharing of the day's bounty remains important to participants. Sitting at long picnic tables, exhausted Mardi Gras and captains relax and review the day's events. Many leave after eating to return home and get cleaned up for the dance at seven o'clock.

The Tee Mamou Dance

The women's dance has been held in various places over the years: dancehalls, a Catholic church hall in Iota, a family res-

taurant in Tee Mamou. A crowd packs the building in anticipation of the arrival of the Mardi Gras.

As they wait, audience members dance to music by a local Cajun band, eat and drink. Shortly before seven o'clock, the Mardi Gras gather outside the hall. Many are wearing new masks and costumes, often more elaborate than their daytime disguises. Suson Launey, for instance, recently made a *bal* mask featuring plastic eyes lit by blinking bulbs. Disguises must be durable as well as decorative, though, because the women at the dance are frequently even more unrestrained in their antics than they were during the day. New costumes replace those that are dirty and torn, and also ensure that captains will not immediately recognize the Mardi Gras.

As the band begins "Le Jig de Mardi Gras," the dance floor is cleared for the guisers' entrance. Side by side, they dance into the hall in pairs and circle the dance floor, whooping and stamping their feet in time to the music. When the tune ends, the *capitaine* calls the Mardi Gras to the middle of the floor. There, they kneel in a circle to sing their Mardi Gras song once more. Singing the final lines requesting a "little something," the Mardi Gras pound the wooden floor with their hands, signaling spectators to shower them with coins.

As they have done throughout the day, the Mardi Gras first dance a fast dance and then a slow waltz, finding partners among

Left, above:
Two Mardi Gras take green onions from a host's garden, 1994.

Left, below:
Two Tee Mamou Mardi Gras beg for coins from onlookers, 1991.

Left, above:
A Mardi Gras hides in a trash barrel, 1993.

Left, below:
A Mardi Gras hides in an ice bin during a visit to a neighborhood store, 1995.

91

Mardi Gras link hands
and legs to prolong
their house visit.

Left, above:
A captain is wrestled to the ground by the Mardi Gras.

Left, below:
Longtime Mardi Gras Merline Bergeaux carrying eggs from a host's barn, 1993.

93

the onlookers. The *capitaine* then signals the group to leave the hall.

What follows is an intensified version of the game that has taken place repeatedly during the run, as the Mardi Gras resist the captains' efforts to eject them. They crawl under tables, climb rafters, and enlist the help of amused spectators who often slip them food and drink. Suson Launey says, "And we will stay there and we won't go out until they stop feeding us and giving us something to drink."

Once a Mardi Gras is discovered, it often takes several captains to pull her from the hall, as she rolls, clings to table legs, and even jumps on captains' backs. A Mardi Gras who is usually among the last to be pulled out describes this longstanding tradition for both the men's and women's runs: "After we finish our dances, we go hide underneath the table and the captain's got to pull us out, you know. We give him a fight, [because] we don't want to go out." Another Mardi Gras says, "And we ain't going easy, let me tell you. They have to take us out. And more than likely the captains are going out, too."

Once chased or dragged out, the Mardi Gras stops struggling and unmasks. When the last straggler has been discovered, the band begins playing again and the crowd resumes dancing. Many Mardi Gras, now undisguised, reenter to visit and dance until it is time to dress again for the next

Tee Mamou Mardi Gras holding a child.

"round." The entire performance is enacted two or three times during the dance.

The women's *courir* ends as the last Mardi Gras is pulled across the line during the final "round" of the dance. Many will not mask again until next year. Others costume once again on Tuesday afternoon, when a group of women meet the men's run on the outskirts of Iota for a triumphant parade through town.

Throughout the year, though, being a Mardi Gras is an important part of their identity. Running Mardi Gras is "in their blood," they say. And Merline Bergeaux, a founder of the women's run, says, "Whenever I die, you can just put my suit, mask and *capuchon* with me."

At their dance, Tee Mamou women resist captains' efforts to drag them from the hall, 1994.

Merline's words apply equally to the extraordinary folk artists who craft the best-loved and most-used Cajun Mardi Gras masks in Basile and Tee Mamou. The greatest maskmakers tend also to be *grands Mardi Gras*, great revelers.

These artists work intently, summoning their creativity and resourcefulness to shape everyday materials and dimestore oddities into palpable images that somehow seem to freeze in their features all the wild energy of Cajun Mardi Gras. But crafting the mask is not enough. The unworn mask is merely a shadow of the use to which it is put on the most special day of the Cajun calendar, when the artists animate their frozen faces. At that special time, maskmakers transform themselves into consummate tricksters and beggars, mounting a daylong drama of songs, dances, foolishness, feasting, and sharing. They tease, scare, and delight their unmasked neighbors—and carry them briefly into a place where the mask becomes a living thing.

95

References

Ancelet, Barry Jean. 1989. *"Capitaine, voyage ton flag": The Traditional Cajun Country Mardi Gras.* Lafayette: Center for Louisiana Studies, University of Southwestern Louisiana.

Kinser, Samuel. 1990. *Carnival, American Style.* Chicago: University of Chicago Press.

Lindahl, Carl. 1996a. "Bakhtin's Carnival Laughter and the Cajun Country Mardi Gras." *Folklore* 107: 49–62.

———. 1996b. "The Presence of the Past in the Cajun Country Mardi Gras." *Journal of Folklore Research* 33: 125–53.

Mire, Pat, director. 1993. *Dance for a Chicken: The Cajun Mardi Gras.* 57 min., 1/2" video format, color. Eunice, LA: Attakapas Productions.

Post, Lauren C. 1974. *Cajun Sketches from the Prairies of Southwest Louisiana.* 2nd ed. Baton Rouge: Louisiana State University Press.

Roshto, Ronnie E. 1992. "Georgie and Allen Manuel and Cajun Wire Screen Masks." *Louisiana Folklore Miscellany* 7: 33–49.

Savoy, Ann. 1984. *Cajun Music: A Reflection of a People.* Eunice, LA: Bluebird Press.

Ware, Carolyn. 1994. "Reading the Rules Backward: Women and the Rural Cajun Mardi Gras." Ph.D. diss., University of Pennsylvania.

———. 1995. "'I Read the Rules Backward': Women, Symbolic Inversion and the Cajun Mardi Gras Run." *Southern Folklore* 52: 137–60.

Maskmakers' Addresses

Many Cajun maskmakers, including some featured in this book, sell their masks. Readers wishing to purchase masks may contact the following artists at the addresses below or may visit the Prairie Acadian Culture Center in Eunice, Louisiana, where Mardi Gras masks are available for sale.

Renée Frugé
5859 Tom Hebert Rd.
Lake Charles, LA 70605

J. B. LeBlue and Family
P. O. Box 367
Basile, LA 70515

Jackie Miller
Rt. 1, Box 396
Iota, LA 70543

Kim Moreau
Rt. 1, Box 1082
Bearcat Rd.
Basile, LA 70515

Suson Launey
P.O. Box 190
Iota, LA 70543

Georgie Manuel, Potpourri
361 West Maple
Eunice, LA 70535

Vories Moreau
244 St. Paul Ave.
Opelousas, LA 70770